White Coat, Black Face

A Doctor's Guide to Overcome Your Emotional Flatline

Pamela Buchanan, MD

ISBN-13: 979-8-9988072-0-6
Library of Congress Control Number: 2025910798

Book cover design by Nathan S.
The Author's Journey Publishing Co.

Dedication

For my children, Zealand, Zurich, and Caren. Thanks for letting me work on this and being such great children as well as my inspiration.

Table of Contents

Get Your Free Guide

The StrongHER Method™
10 Ways to Banish Stress for Good

How It Works:

01 Scan the QR Code
Open your camera or QR code scanning app and point it at the code below.

02 Provide Your Email
Subscribe to the StrongHer email list to receive your free guide. Be sure to confirm your subscription.

03 Look Out for Invite
Check your email for an invite to the STrongHer Purpose Circle.

Having trouble with the QR Code?
Try this: https://bit.ly/4cRQRn3

Foreword

When I first entered the world of healthcare, it was from a place of understanding and care, as a physical therapist dedicated to helping people heal. In recent years, I've also become a patient, experiencing firsthand the challenges of the medical system. Through my journey, I've come to realize that we must extend our support to doctors, not only because they care for our health, but also because their well-being is intrinsically linked to our own.

As a healthcare professional and someone who has battled cancer three times in just two years, I know the weight of navigating both the physical and emotional challenges of illness. What I didn't anticipate, however, was the profound grief and sense of loss I felt upon learning that one of my trusted doctors had taken his own life.

In that moment, I felt the weight of his absence, not just for myself but for the thousands of patients who had lost a doctor they trusted, someone who had made a life-changing difference in their care, and in my own. I wasn't alone in feeling the grief. I came to understand that approximately one doctor dies by suicide every day—this is not just a personal loss but a systemic crisis within the medical field.

Doctors are under immense pressure, facing mounting administrative burdens, moral distress, and, tragically, a lack of systemic support. This doesn't just impact physicians; it affects us all. When a doctor takes their own life, thousands of patients are left without care, creating a ripple effect that can be devastating. A good doctor is irreplaceable. And yet, we ask these same doctors to carry enormous responsibilities with limited resources, often in environments that don't foster their well-being.

I've spent countless hours in conversation with physicians, some who have contemplated suicide, some who have survived suicide attempts, and even spouses of doctors who have died from suicide. This is a stark and painful reality that we cannot ignore! The toll on our doctors is real, and it's affecting our healthcare system in profound ways. More than half of physicians are experiencing burnout, which is directly linked to poorer patient outcomes. When you feel depleted, it's impossible to perform at your best and provide the best care. This is the reality for many physicians right now. They are human, too. And they are silently crying out for our support.

Dr. Kathy Stepien said, "Everyone wins when physicians are well." It's a simple truth; doctors are people, too. They experience stress, fear, frustration, and sadness just like anyone else. They are not invincible or superhuman, and they need our empathy, our kindness, and our support.

If you want your doctor to be there for you, you need to understand the challenges they face. Kindness is a powerful tool we all can offer. It doesn't have to be complicated. A simple "thank you," a gesture of appreciation, or a moment to let your doctor know they are valued can make a world of difference.

We need to address the systemic issues that contribute to burnout and distress as well. Overwhelming workloads, administrative hurdles, and moral injury are just a few of the contributors to a healthcare environment that leaves physicians vulnerable.

The physician crisis we are facing requires all of us to step up, not just in caring for our doctors but in ensuring that they have the resources, systems, and support they need to thrive. This is not just about caring for physicians; it's about protecting the heart of our healthcare system, our doctors, and ensuring that they are able to care for us when we need them most.

In the pages of this book, you'll hear from a doctor who has walked through the darkness of contemplating suicide, who has faced the emotional flatline, and who continues to navigate the complexities of healing not only her patients but herself. Dr. Pamela Buchanan's bravery in sharing her story is a powerful reminder of the importance of taking care of those who care for us.

I have made it my mission to support doctors in any way I can. I listen to them. I amplify their voices and build a sense of community through my "Stand Up (for) Doctors!" YouTube channel and Substack newsletter, as well as LinkedIn posts. I invite others to join me in showing support to help ease the burden on the medical professionals who dedicate their lives to helping others.

The fight against physician burnout and suicide requires a collective effort. As patients, we can make a difference. We can be the support our doctors so desperately need. Let's Stand Up for Doctors!

Kim Downey
Physical Therapist
Stand Up (for) Doctors!
Community Ambassador for Medicine Forward & Dr. Lorna Breen Heroes' Foundation

PART 1

The Emotional Flatline

Chapter 1

The Doctor Is In (And Always Was)

Don't wait around for other people to be happy for you.
Any happiness you get, you've got to make yourself.

—Alice Walker

Since the age of 12, I've wanted to be a doctor. In my family, trips to the doctor's office were always a treat. The night before, Mom would press my hair and make two ponytails with rollers at the end. The next day, she'd add ribbons or ballies, and I'd put on a cute dress and shoes. Afterwards, if it was a school day—and if I behaved—she would take me to get something to eat. Back then, trips to McDonald's, Burger King, or Best Steakhouse were just a few of the rewards.

We were poor, and I loved going to the doctor. My favorite was pediatrician Dr. Helen Nash. She was so inspirational. Her office was located in the hood, and the brick building reminded me of the TV show *Good Times*. Ironically, I eventually worked in a free clinic that resembled that building.

Inside, the waiting room looked like someone's living room. It had red walls with cute little paintings and magazines neatly fanned out across coffee tables. Also, there was a donut shop across the street. Stopping there became another reward for visiting the doctor—and it was probably my favorite. You couldn't get donuts like that in the suburbs.

I was never afraid of doctor visits or even getting shots because Mom made every trip feel like a treat. Also, Dr. Nash and her staff were warm and kind, and Dr. Nash would take time to encourage me to stay out of trouble and get an education. She would tell me I was a smart girl. To a young girl who was teased for being "slow," that meant a lot.

They were such great memories; I've kept the tradition going with my own kids. They understand that going to the doctor was more than a medical necessity;

it was a special occasion wrapped with tradition. And they know, just like I did, that a special lunch always comes next. As a doctor, I try to carry the same comfort my mother embodied and make each visit a positive experience for my young patients, just as Dr. Nash did for me.

Success and Challenges in the ER

With almost two decades of practice, I can say that I've been pretty successful. I started out in private practice but transitioned to emergency medicine for the shift work hours and better pay. My career has not only flourished, but I've also been routinely praised by patients young and old. I'm doing what I love and never desired to do anything else.

As an emergency room (ER) doctor, we are taught to "treat and street" patients. Colleagues jokingly refer to us as "whores of medicine" because we have no relationships with patients. We are in triage mode when it's busy, and the system is not designed for us to be primary care, although many people use the ER that way. We take a few minutes to make a diagnosis then refer the patient for continuity of care. That was part of the allure for me. No after-hours call. When the shift is over, it's over.

Now sadly, the ER is referred to as the garbage can of medicine. These days, patients are angry because they wait too long in a stress-filled, understaffed emergency room, and they take their frustrations out on us. When we're having a good day, they're discharged within a couple of hours. They're either given a prescription and directions to follow up with their primary care physician, or if they're really sick, we send them upstairs to the hospital. But on a typical day, just waiting to be seen can be longer than a couple of hours.

I worked 12-hour to 24-hour shifts, often getting little to no sleep, and struggled to maintain a work-life balance. The challenges of the ER are that we have to see everyone. It's the law. And there are people who abuse the system and come weekly for the same issue. We know they don't have a medical problem, but we must see them anyway. Some of these people are violent or psychotic, so I am constantly worried about safety.

Recently, someone threatened to come back and harm me, and has called the hospital to see when

I'm on shift. This has caused me to work days only, and I'm extra careful when walking into and out of the hospital.

In an effort to spend more time with my children, I chose to work at a rural hospital one and a half hours away from home. Also, the pay was better. In addition to the 12-24 hour shifts, I also had a one and a half hour commute to and from work. But after more than ten years of commuting to and working in the ER, everything gradually started to weigh on my emotional health—I was on the path to burnout. The Agency for Healthcare Quality and Research (2017) describes physician burnout as a long-term stress reaction marked by emotional exhaustion, depersonalization, and a lacking sense of personal accomplishment due to packed workdays, the demanding pace, time pressures, and emotional intensity.

In addition, the long hours and commute meant I missed important moments in my children's lives, and I knew I couldn't get them back. I was a mother of three, and one of my sons was diagnosed with Crohn's disease. Soon after taking this role, all I could ever think about was home. I was losing out on priceless family moments that I could never relive. I missed games, PTA meetings, everything. When my daughter's senior tennis night came and went without me, she said, "It's okay, Mom," her voice tinged with the disappointment she tried to hide. "I know your work is important." Those words stung more than any rebuke. I knew it wasn't okay, and I'd spend the rest of my life making it up to her.

Despite loving what I do, I started to feel agitated, and it wasn't long before self-doubt, a common symptom of burnout, crept in. I found myself second-guessing decisions I made thousands of times before, even routine ones. The once-comforting feel of my stethoscope started to feel like a noose.

In addition, the harsh fluorescent lights of the ER had never bothered me before, but they had started to blur into one continuous glare, causing eye strain. Sleep became a luxury, and real meals became a distant memory. The acrid taste of energy drinks and protein shakes had become substitutes for the four main food groups, barely masking the tang of exhaustion on my tongue.

Instead of addressing these thoughts and feelings, I dismissed them, convincing myself that they were a normal part of life for an ER doctor. But, like a patient ignoring the warning signs of heart disease, I was setting myself up for a crisis. Little did I know that another crisis, a global crisis, was just around the corner.

COVID Burnout

The COVID-19 pandemic hit the medical community like a massive heart attack and transformed the ER into a warzone, the air thick with fear and the sharp, bitter, artificial smell of disinfectant. I felt like a soldier on the battlefield running out of ammunition. The weight of my quarantine protection gear—the N95 respirator, face shield, boot covers, hood, and gloves—was heavy but offered little protection against the enemy.

As you may recall, the rural community strongly resisted precautionary measures and often criticized those who followed them. During COVID, I witnessed this resistance all too frequently. Despite our best efforts, we simply couldn't reach many of them in time. For example, during the start of the quarantine, a couple held their wedding anyway, an event we dubbed the "Red Wedding." It included guests from the neighboring towns of Cypress and Cedar Hills, and before the wedding, the ER was relatively quiet. Residents were even saying, "See? COVID isn't that bad."

The bride was an obese white woman with plain brown hair, and the groom was lanky and endearingly awkward-looking with a blondish-brown buzz cut. The bridesmaids' dresses were magenta, hence the name "Red Wedding." A few days after the nuptials, a little old man came in with a cough and sniffles. Then the best man followed, feeling seriously ill, and it snowballed from there. The ER became overwhelmed for the next five to six months. Despite the worsening situation—illness, job loss, death—the townspeople insisted on living their lives as usual.

Ignorance about the virus spread just as quickly as the disease, often tinged with racism and xenophobia. There were people who called and asked if eating Chinese food gave them the "Wuhan flu," and they were as serious as cancer. We also had patients who refused care from our Filipino or Asian nurses out of fear of contracting COVID-19 from them.

I was the medical director and the only Black doctor in the workplace, and I felt isolated and constantly on edge. When patients noticed that I was treating them, some would ask for another doctor or the supervisor. Each time, I calmly explained that I was the only option, and every time, I was met with racial slurs, surprise, or refusals to be treated by me.

This went on for months. Every interaction was contentious and political, with patients slurring racial epithets at me and the staff, questioning my abilities, or simply surprised that I spoke well. Many antagonized me about masks and other preventive measures, and I found myself working to avoid arguments. When the subject of COVID came up, I simply stated that I wore a mask and hadn't contracted COVID-19, then focused on doing my job and getting out of there.

It wasn't long after the Red Wedding that every ER patient's vitals were dangerously unstable. It was chaos—alarms blaring constantly and machines wailing like sirens, warning us that something was terribly wrong. The truth was, everything was wrong.

Before COVID, those alarms were manageable. They would only go off occasionally. In the ER, you'd have maybe two or three patients hooked up to a monitor at any given time, and those alarms were useful. When we heard the alarms go off, it meant we could respond, triage, stabilize a patient, and move on. I longed for the days of being a prostitute doctor.

But during COVID, I couldn't rely on those alarms anymore because they all screamed at once. The constant noise became white noise, and it was impossible to tell the difference between what was urgent and what was catastrophic.

It was terrifying. So, I had to create my own mental triage system and make gut-wrenching decisions. Who was most likely to make it? Who wasn't? Which patient had the best chance of survival? Is it the 85-year-old with asthma but otherwise healthy or the 35-year-old with multiple chronic conditions? You're forced to choose, knowing full well that someone might not make it because you couldn't be everywhere at once.

I'll never forget one of the worst nights. There were so many patients in the ER. People were gasping for air and struggling with every breath. At one point, I stood still, feeling frozen in place. I had eight patients, all in varying degrees of crisis, and only one me. The exhaustion was unlike anything I'd ever felt before. It wasn't just physical—it was mental and emotional depletion on a level I couldn't even process. I had to choose who to save.

And then came the worst sound of all: flatline. As patients were dying and being put on ventilators, they would ask for vaccines as a last resort. I had to explain that it wouldn't help at that stage; vaccines were effective for those who hadn't contracted COVID-19. This took an emotional toll on me, driving me to a dark place where I questioned my own care for those who didn't believe in the virus's severity.

One night, after losing two patients in a single shift, I retreated to my call room. The silence was a stark contrast to the ER's constant cacophony. I broke down, tears streaming down my face. The full weight of everything hit me, crushing my chest and making it difficult for me to breathe; it was a panic attack. I felt utterly useless, a fraud in a white coat. The passion that once drove me to medicine had flatlined completely.

I'd always been someone who could handle stress, or at least that's what I told myself. I'd been through a lot in my life, and I always found a way to keep moving forward. But the pandemic changed everything. It wasn't just the fear of the virus or the exhaustion from the long hours—it was the isolation. Despite the world coming to a halt and everyone staying at home, I remained an "essential worker." That meant I had no choice but to keep showing up, even when I felt like I couldn't anymore.

I experienced a level of isolation that I had never experienced before. I was unable to spend time with my children in the way I desired. To mitigate the risk of exposing them to COVID, I lived in the room above our garage, keeping my distance but yearning for a hug.

Every day, after my 12- or 24-hour shift, I'd drive one and a half hours home and strip down in the garage to shower. With my son on immunosuppressants for Crohn's disease, the fear of bringing the virus home to my children never left me. So for months, I didn't see my children but would hear them in the house talking, laughing, and playing. I couldn't touch them, couldn't sit with them, couldn't breathe around them, and couldn't be the mom they needed and I wanted to be.

Have you ever been afraid you would kill your child by just breathing on him? The thought of hurting my children by bringing this deadly virus into my home was unbearable, so I remained isolated and worked more hours. The hours piled up even more because I never contracted COVID and would fill in for those who were out sick. But staying away from my family was making me depressed.

Driving to work through empty streets was a strange, almost surreal experience that amplified my sense of isolation. It reminded me of an apocalyptic movie. The normally bustling roads were now eerily silent, stripped of their usual morning chaos—no rush-hour traffic, no school buses, no commuters hurrying to their jobs. Each mile felt like traversing a landscape between reality and some dystopian nightmare.

The emptiness was more than a visual phenomenon; it was a visceral representation of collective fear and withdrawal. Storefronts stood dark, their windows reflecting my vehicle like blank, unseeing eyes. Parking lots that would typically be filled with cars sat as expansive, desolate concrete plains. Traffic signals changed colors with robotic precision, mechanically obedient, indifferent to the stillness.

I knew mental health mattered. I knew, logically, that this too would pass. But I couldn't admit I wasn't okay. It felt like the movie *Groundhog's Day*, only darker—no jokes, no do-overs—just a loop of pain with no exit. Drive 1.5 hours. Work 24. Get called a nigger bitch. Watch people die. Drive 1.5 hours. Work 24. Get called a nigger bitch. Watch people die. Drive 1.5 hours.

At the height of the pandemic, I'd cross a long steel bridge over the Missouri River, the streets behind me a ghost town, the road ahead empty. I dreaded both destinations—work and home. At work, death. At home, loneliness. And every day, as the virus claimed more lives and loneliness claimed what was left of me, I'd cross that bridge with the same thought echoing in my head: Jump. Just jump.

Chapter 2

Code Blue for the Soul

You don't have to control your thoughts. You just have to stop letting them control you.

—Dr. Judson Brewer, psychiatrist & neuroscientist

———————————————————————————

The thing about depression is that it doesn't care about logic or reason. It sneaks in quietly, like a shadow slipping under the door, and takes hold of you, no matter how "good" life might look from the outside.

And I wasn't alone. There were countless other healthcare professionals who silently carried the weight of the world on their shoulders. Burnout became a shared affliction with no mental health resources offered and no debriefing after a particularly brutal shift. The hospital was quick to shove a swab up my nose if I so much as sneezed, but no one ever asked, "Are you okay?" To truly understand the lack of compassion shown to healthcare workers, let me share a few stories I've had to process on my own.

Unforgettable Cases

Early in my career, a man came into the ER after being electrocuted by a power line. He was a lineman, and the electricity had scorched him so badly that his skin looked like charcoal. His back was blackened and swollen, puffed up from the burns. We had to perform an escharotomy—a procedure where you make deep cuts into the burned skin to relieve pressure and allow the body to breathe.

I'll never forget the sound when the scalpel sliced through his burned flesh. It was horrifyingly similar to the sound of cutting into a brisket when you let it rest after cooking. Then there was the smell—an acrid, sickly scent that lingered far longer than it should have. We worked on him, knowing, deep down, that he wasn't going to survive. He was too far gone.

Even now, 17 years later, I can't barbecue with charcoal. I have a pellet grill because I can't bear the sight of charcoal briquettes. Every time I see them, I'm transported back to that day in the ER, the sounds, the smells, and the overwhelming sense of helplessness. That image haunted my dreams for years and still lingers in the back of my mind.

One of the worst cases I ever worked on was a man who'd been in a motorcycle accident. By the time he came to us, he was nearly decapitated—his head was barely attached, held on by a thin strip of skin.

I remember having to manipulate his head to see if there was anything we could do. As I turned it, his head almost rolled off the table. It was like something out of a horror movie. I had to fight to stay composed, to focus on the task at hand. There was no mandatory counseling after that. No one sat me down to process the sheer trauma of handling something so gruesome.

But that's the thing about working in the ER—what you see sticks with you. You don't just walk away from cases like that and go back to normal. You carry it with you, whether you want to or not.

These stories occurred before COVID and had contributed to my burnout and depression. And during the height of the pandemic, there were several more cases that added to it, and eventually, an emotional flatline. Here's one that stuck with me for months.

Nursing home residents were among the hardest hit. We treated so many elderly patients with COVID, and most of them didn't survive. But there was one patient I'll never forget. She was frail and gaunt, her body ravaged by age and illness. She looked like something out of a horror movie—like the Crypt Keeper, with sunken eyes and skin stretched tight over her bones.

As she was dying, she grabbed my arm with what little strength she had left. Her grip was weak, but the moment was powerful. I could feel the life draining out of her, her energy slipping away as she looked at me with fear and desperation.

For months, I couldn't shake the feeling of her touch. In my dreams, I'd see her crawling across the floor, like the girl from *The Ring*, grabbing at my leg and pulling me down. I'd wake up kicking and gasping for air, still trapped in the nightmare.

What makes these stories harder to bear is the lack of support for people like me—ER doctors and nurses who are exposed to horrors like this every day. Paramedics and police officers who bring these patients to us have mandatory counseling before they're allowed to return to work.

But in the ER? We don't get that. No one checks in on us after a bad call. No one asks how we're doing or whether we're okay when those moments stay with us. It wasn't just the incidents that wore on us. It was also the silence that followed them. I didn't talk about what I'd seen or how I felt, and no one asked or spoke about how it made them feel. The weight kept piling up until I couldn't tell the difference between normal stress and something far more dangerous. It wasn't a burnout. It wasn't depression. It was something I didn't yet have language for.

The Insidious Nature of the Emotional Flatline

An emotional flatline doesn't barge in like a fire. It seeps in like carbon monoxide—quiet, invisible, lethal. It starts with small things. You ignore fatigue, burnout, and depression. You rationalize the constant tension in your shoulders. You normalize skipping meals, skipping sleep, skipping joy. You think, "This is just what it takes."

And for a while, it is. I loved being a doctor and didn't take issue with all of its demands. I felt honored every time I walked into a room and someone trusted me with their life or the life of someone they loved. I never took that for granted.

That said, it wasn't easy getting here, getting to an emotional flatline. I fought through the whispers of people calling me slow before we understood why. I stood toe-to-toe with sexism that told me I was too emotional, too soft, too loud, too much. I stared racism in the face—sometimes subtle, sometimes sharp—and refused to let it decide who I could become. I failed more than once. But I got back up every time. Becoming a doctor was my dream, and I lived it fully. I didn't want to give up.

But somewhere along the way, the dream shifted. The call room started to feel like a cage. The stethoscope around my neck felt heavier. I could do everything I was trained to do—intubate, resuscitate, diagnose, lead a code—but I couldn't *feel* it anymore.

The highs didn't lift me. The lows didn't faze me. I wasn't tired; I was numb. I wasn't broken; I was blank.

That's what no one tells you. The emotional flatline doesn't scream—it whispers. It disguises itself as discipline, as hustle, as sacrifice. And by the time you realize you're drowning, you've already gone under.

Deep down, I knew I needed to define it because it was more than exhaustion, burnout, or depression. And naming it meant I could dissect its parts and find a cure. So I defined emotional flatline as:

A clinical and cultural phenomenon marked by the chronic suppression of one's emotional needs in response to prolonged stress, trauma, or role-based overfunctioning. Common among high-achieving professionals—particularly those in caregiving, mission-driven, or marginalized roles—this state is not defined by sadness or despair but by emotional numbness disguised as composure. The emotional flatline presents as quiet endurance, blunted joy, and a dangerous normalization of self-neglect. It is not the absence of emotion, but the strategic silencing of it for the sake of survival, perceived strength, or societal expectation. Left unaddressed, it erodes identity, purpose, and mental health—one silent heartbeat at a time.

I wasn't going to stay there because I refused to give up my dream of being a doctor. But it took another incident for me to finally seek help.

Losing a Mentor to the Pandemic's Toll

This doctor seemed to have it all, the kind of person who could light up a room—a real happy-go-lucky type, like Robin Williams. But just like Robin, he carried a pain no one could see.

To me, he was more than a colleague —he was a guiding star in the chaotic early years of my career. He taught me to navigate medicine with purpose and integrity. His energy was infectious, and he had this incredible way of making everyone feel seen, valued, and capable.

During residency on my ER rotation, when days blurred into nights and exhaustion was my constant companion, his words were often the only thing keeping me going.

"Take it one patient at a time," he'd say, his voice steady and calm, even in the middle of the ER chaos. "You can't save everyone, but you can always make someone's day better."

For that, I admired him deeply. He wasn't just a brilliant doctor—he was a father, a husband, and a pillar in his church. He played guitar in the worship band on Sundays and could bring humor into even the most tense situations.

But even the brightest lights have shadows. I first noticed something was off during my residency. He took an extended leave, and while rumors swirled among the staff, no one dared to ask him what was going on. When he returned, he seemed quieter, a little more withdrawn, but still kind and supportive. It wasn't until years later, when I worked with him at his standalone urgent care, that I learned the truth.

One night, after a particularly long shift, we were sitting in the break room, sipping lukewarm coffee and decompressing.

"I broke my back years ago," he said, almost casually. "Got hooked on pain pills during recovery. Rehab helped, but... it's a fight every day."

I was stunned. He didn't seem like someone who struggled with anything. To me, he was the epitome of resilience and composure—or at least that's what I thought.

"You'd never guess it," he said with a tired smile. "And that's the problem. People see what they want to see."

His words stuck with me. Even though I didn't fully understand the weight he carried, I admired his honesty and the fact that he kept showing up, even when it was hard.

But the pandemic stretched us all to our breaking points, and he was no exception. Running a standalone urgent care during such a chaotic time was grueling. Financial pressures mounted, patients were relentless, and the days seemed never-ending.

Still, he tried to stay positive. He posted inspirational messages on Facebook almost daily, urging everyone to "keep your head up" and "stay strong." I found comfort in his words, thinking that if he could stay optimistic, so could I.

Then one morning, I overheard a nurse speaking in hushed tones. "Did you hear about him?" she asked. "I can't believe it."

My heart sank. I felt my stomach twist as I demanded to know what had happened. "He's gone," she said softly. "He took his own life."

I felt like I'd been punched in the chest. It didn't make sense. How could someone so strong and so capable feel so hopeless? I replayed every interaction in my mind, searching for signs I might have missed.

I learned later that he'd been struggling more than anyone knew. The financial pressures of running the urgent care, his history of addiction, and the relentless stress of the pandemic had become too much.

In the weeks that followed, I couldn't shake the guilt. I kept asking myself if there was something that could have been done, some way the system could have helped him. I thought about his family, his children, his patients—everyone who had relied on him. And then I wondered, "If someone like him could feel that hopeless, what hope is there for the rest of us?"

His death forced me to confront my own breaking point. The pandemic had taken its toll on me too, and I could feel the cracks in my own mental health growing wider. For the first time, I realized I couldn't keep carrying it all on my own. I wasn't okay, and I finally had to admit that to myself.

Chapter 3

Unmasked: The Day I Asked for Help

Even the strongest among us need support.

—Dr. Nadine Burke Harris

I wasn't well for a while and resisted therapy for so long because I thought it was for people who weren't strong enough to handle life's challenges on their own. And I was supposed to be strong. I was the one who helped others, not the one who needed help. But losing my mentor changed that. His death shattered my sense of control. It made me confront a truth I'd been avoiding: even the strongest among us need support.

When it came time to look for a therapist, the first hurdle was just finding one. That process was a trial all on its own. I started by doing what I always recommend to my patients: I looked at the back of my insurance card and called the number for guidance, and my insurance company gave me a list of five providers. But one by one, each of them said the same thing: "We don't take that insurance." Insurance companies can be notoriously difficult to work with; it felt like they were trying to trick me at every turn.

Eventually, I found a therapist I thought would take my insurance. But when I sat down for my first session, she told me, "We don't take your insurance." I felt frustrated and defeated. I was already there, so I decided to pay for it out of pocket. It was money I didn't really have to spare, but I told myself it was an investment in my well-being. Still, the whole ordeal left me wondering: Why is getting help so hard? For someone already struggling with their mental health, these barriers are almost enough to make you give up.

Unpacking Layers of Pain

I wasn't sure what to expect during the session, but the way it worked was surprising to me. Therapy wasn't some rigid, formal process. It felt more like having a conversation. We'd just talk, and then my therapist would say, "Next time you're in a situation like that, here's what I want you to do." It was informal and almost unstructured, but it worked. She gave me tools and strategies to use when I was feeling overwhelmed—practical things I could actually apply in the moment.

What really helped, though, was how she made me feel about my emotions. She'd listen as I poured my heart out and then tell me, "It's okay to feel what you feel. It's not abnormal. I hear it all the time." That acknowledgment made me feel seen, like I wasn't alone in this. She even said, "A lot of people like you—doctors, especially—are like this." Hearing that from her gave me a sense of comfort and hope, as if I was finally doing something about my mental health.

The sessions forced me to unpack my grief, my guilt, and the immense pressure I placed on myself. It taught me how to set boundaries, prioritize self-care, and most importantly, accept that it's okay to not be okay.

But it also forced me to confront how the pandemic intensified everything—the isolation, the depression, the racial tension—and pushed me deeper into an emotional flatline. This wasn't a single traumatic moment, but the slow, quiet outcome of carrying too much for too long—until even my emotional responses felt muted by design.

Emotional flatline is more than exhaustion; it's a chronic adaptation to trauma, stress, and overfunctioning, especially in caregiving or marginalized roles. It's not the immediate wound of trauma, but the long-term silencing that follows—a dangerous numbness disguised as composure.

Trauma Soundtrack

Dr. Gabor Maté says that "trauma is not what happens to you; it's what happens inside you as a result of what happens to you (CBC 2022)." For a doctor, this means that while a traumatic event—like the death of a patient—may occur during practice, the true trauma lies in the internal response to that event. It's the guilt, the helplessness, and the anxiety that follow, far more than the event itself.

Trauma in medicine isn't always about a single moment. It's the internalized impact of countless experiences—each one interpreted, processed, and absorbed differently. Even when we know the outcomes aren't in our control, the emotional weight of these situations takes a toll. Then there's vicarious trauma, the result of witnessing others' suffering day after day, which accumulates over time and creates a profound emotional strain.

There was a soundtrack to my trauma, the barrage of alarms from patients' heart monitors. The machines had become extensions of my own heartbeat, their constant blip, blip, blip, and meee-row, meee-row of emergency alerts embedding themselves into my psyche. The sounds didn't stop when the shift or scene ended. They followed me home. And without the chance to hug my children or find comfort in my family, those sounds followed me into my dreams. Just like the countless other healthcare providers, I kept going, shift after shift, carrying the loneliness and the weight of all the lives I couldn't save and the trauma I couldn't escape.

Racism in the ER and the Anatomy of My Emotional Flatline

I don't know why I did not realize earlier that a big part of my burnout was due to racism. It was always there, but it became amplified after the 2020 presidential election. Politics had completely infiltrated medicine like never before. People were mean and disrespectful.

There was one patient I'll never forget. He was in a wheelchair, quadriplegic, and clearly a heavy smoker. The ER was packed that day, and I was running from room to room. I stopped by his room, did my exam, ran the COVID test, and came back with the results. I explained his treatment plan—Decadron, breathing treatments, maybe remdesivir. He was only half-listening because he was on the phone with someone.

As I walked out of his room, I heard him say loud and clear, "The nigger bitch doctor says I got COVID."

The nurses froze. One of them asked me, "Did I hear what I think I just heard?"

I waved it off. "Calm down; it's not the first time I have been called that, and it won't be the last."

Seemingly unbothered, I went back in to finish his treatment, and he was coughing and wheezing, still trying to argue with me.

"I don't have COVID," he insisted.

"You have COVID," I said calmly.

"No, I don't. You have COVID," he shot back.

I sighed and said, "Sir, we're not going back and forth. You have COVID. Here's the treatment."

The steroids helped, and once he could breathe better, we transferred him to the main hospital. As they wheeled him out, he looked at me and said, "I'm sorry. I didn't mean that. That's not who I am."

I stopped, looked him in the eye, and said, "You absolutely did mean it. That's absolutely who you are. Own it! Do better."

I heard later that he went to the floor and called the other Black doctor, the hospitalist, the same thing. I knew his apology was empty.

Before COVID, I could only recall one other time I'd been called the n-word at work. It happened when I was a resident. An older white man came into the ER after a car accident, and he was having a heart attack. Even as a resident, I was in charge of ordering the medications, so I ordered morphine for his heart attack and did all the usual procedures. While I was attending to him, he grabbed my hand, stroked it, and said, "You're the nicest nigger I've ever met." I immediately thought, "Oh my God. That really happened." Not knowing how to respond, I continued with his care.

What made it almost ironic was that morning before I left for work, I had been staying with my parents. At the time, my husband, my toddler daughter, and I were in between houses, waiting for ours to be ready for move-in. As I was getting ready for work, my mom said to me, "Don't let the crackers get you down today."

My mom grew up in Mississippi, the real Mississippi. Her family moved north after a lynching. My dad's farm was next to hers, and their families migrated separately—my dad's to St. Louis and my mom's to Chicago. She carried those experiences with her and had her opinions about white people, opinions I didn't always agree with. But that day, her words stuck with me.

After that man said what he said, all I could think about was my mom. When I got home, I told her, "The crackers got me down today."

What's interesting about racism is that not every instance is overt or malicious. Some moments were so subtle they almost seemed innocent, but they still carried the weight of ignorance and bias.

One time, I was treating a little baby—maybe 18 months old—and she was staring at me with this wide-eyed curiosity, almost as if I were the strangest thing she'd ever seen. Her mom noticed and chuckled nervously. "Well," she said, "she ain't never seen anybody with dark skin like yours."

I smiled, but inside, I was struck by her words. "Where have y'all been?" I wondered. It was such a small comment, but it carried so much weight about the isolation in some communities, the barriers between people, and how early biases can start to form, even unintentionally.

With therapy, I was unpacking these stories, the layers of pain I hadn't fully acknowledged, the emotional scars left after every slur, as well as the anger that came with patients' refusal to work with the "nigger doctor." As a doctor in a rural hospital, it was occurring way too often, and it was impossible to ignore the emotional toll, the fear of violence, and the weight of being "other" in every space I walked into. Even simple errands led to a gauntlet of stares and tension, bringing up painful and awkward memories from my childhood.

PART 2
Resuscitation

Chapter 4

Not a Diversity Hire—A Dedicated, Educated and Innovative Doctor

When and where I enter... the whole Negro race enters with me.

—Anna Julia Cooper

I've been called a lot of things. Brilliant. Calm under pressure. A badass. But one thing I will never allow myself to be called—not without a response—is a diversity hire.

Let's get one thing straight: I didn't get here because I checked a box. I got here because I passed the same boards and made it through the same sleepless nights, intubated the same crashing patients, and stood in the same trauma rooms with blood on my scrubs and fire in my chest. And I stayed.

Let's talk about staying. Diversity might open a door, but it will never keep you in the room. Especially not in medicine. Especially not as a Black woman.

I think about that cold Missouri night in the ER—rural, under-resourced, flu season at its worst. That shift had already wrung me dry. I had intubated, admitted, stabilized. One younger patient with chronic illnesses needed a central line and an ICU bed—I got the bed. But the doctor coming in after me, a white male colleague, wasn't comfortable doing the procedure. So what did I do?

I stayed over. An hour past the end of my shift. Not just to put in that central line, but to sew up a scared little kid's laceration too. I did it all without flinching because the patient needed me. But when I got in the car afterward, I saw red. I was exhausted and angry—not just because of the work, but because of the weight.

If I had been the one to say I couldn't do a central line... would they have offered me grace? Or would they report me? Fire me? Pull my hospital privileges? Would they say I wasn't qualified? Would they quietly whisper that I only got the job because I was Black and female?

The Political Lie of the "Diversity Hire"

Let's talk about this lie that keeps getting broadcasted on TV screens, podcasts, and YouTube channels—led by men who've never touched a stethoscope or saved a life.

Tucker Carlson once questioned the qualifications of Black female surgeons—calling into doubt whether they were as competent as their peers. The irony? The bar to become a Black female surgeon isn't lower—it's twice as high.

You want to talk about qualifications? Try making it through med school while navigating racism, sexism, and microaggressions that your peers will never understand. Try showing up to a hospital every day where no one looks like you and still perform at the highest level. Try being the only one—and never being allowed to be mediocre.

What Diversity Actually Looks Like

We work harder. We study longer. We show up to more conferences. We worry more. We don't just have to be great. We have to be perfect—because the world is watching and waiting for us to make a mistake.

The exams we take? They're not written in our voice. The language, references, and assumptions—they weren't made with us in mind. We're expected to pass anyway. And we do. Because we must.

Let me be clear: I am not a DEI hire. I am dedicated, educated, and innovative. And I know dozens—hundreds—of Black women in medicine who are the same.

There is nothing deficient about us. There is nothing accidental about our presence. We earned this. With sweat, tears, and sleepless nights.

The Truth About Staying Power

Think about what it takes to become a Black female surgeon. The coursework. The 80-hour weeks. The residents who question your intelligence. The attendings who ignore you. The colleagues who mistake you for a nurse—or worse, a tech—or worse, nobody at all.

Then think about what it takes to stay. Because again, diversity might get you in the door, but only excellence keeps you in the room.

The women I know? They are walking miracles. Not because of their race or gender—but because of their brilliance in spite of what the world throws at them every day.

I walk into every room knowing that my presence shifts the narrative. As Anna Julia Cooper said, "When and where I enter... my race enters with me." I don't carry that lightly. But I also don't carry it alone.

Because every time I put on my white coat, every time I introduce myself as Dr. Buchanan, and every time I save a life, I'm not just answering the call—I'm rewriting what's possible.

And no matter what Tucker Carlson says, I'll be here—thriving, leading, and proving him wrong. One central line at a time.

The Childhood Connection

Diversity also includes disability, both seen and unseen. When I was a child, I took things literally. If someone said, "Don't talk to strangers," I wouldn't talk to strangers. I'd be with my mom, and a new person would say, "Hey, little girl, how are you?" and I'd say nothing because, well, Mom said not to talk to strangers. So that's what I did. Then my mom would tell me, "Don't be rude!" and I'd be thinking, "But you said not to talk to strangers! That's on you, not me!"

Also, if my mom called me and I didn't answer the way people thought was "appropriate," they'd ask, "What's wrong with her? Is she slow or something?"

That happened a lot between the ages of five and ten. And I didn't understand why people thought there was something wrong with me—and why, out of all of my siblings, I was the one going to that man's office.

Every week, my mom took me to that man's office for inkblot tests. I didn't realize at the time that it was a therapy session; I just remember his sweater vest. He showed me cards with inkblots on them and asked, "What do you see?" Every single time, I saw something dead—a dead bunny, a dead dog, a dead bug. To this day, I don't recall whether my mom or that man told me what it meant.

Because of those appointments and the constant criticism for being different, by the time I was 11 or 12, I started to figure out how to act "normal" so I wouldn't stand out. But it only worked so much. I still didn't like to do any social activities. I hated certain smells, touches, fabrics, and I didn't like people touching me. Going to a sleepover? That was a no-go for me. I despised the stares and tension and mindless chatter. No matter how hard I tried, I just didn't fit in.

But my mom didn't see it that way. She thought if I just tried harder, I'd get over it. So, she kept trying to "fix" me, pushing me into activities that were supposed to help me be more social. Cheerleading? Hated those girls. Girl Scouts? Hated them. Church choir? I loathed it. I felt trapped, like I was constantly being forced into these little boxes that didn't fit in order to spend time with kids who constantly made fun of me.

The shame I felt was overwhelming, and it wasn't just about not fitting in—it was about feeling like there was something fundamentally wrong with me.

Like I wasn't enough, or I wasn't "normal." It stayed with me for a long time, and even now, I sometimes catch myself questioning whether I'm doing enough to fit in with the world's expectations.

Back in the late '80s and early '90s when I was dealing with all of this, they weren't calling my difference anything specific. At first, they thought I had a learning disability, but testing had ruled that out. Then they suggested it was more of a processing issue, which is why I started seeing that man. But no one ever gave it a clear name until I was older.

Chapter 5

Different, Not Defective

Being different is not a disease. It's a declaration that you were made for something uncommon.

—Dr. Thema Bryant, psychologist, minister, and president of the American Psychological Association

---

Later in life, I realized that the man my mother took me to see was a therapist, and he had explained to my mom that I had Asperger's Syndrome, a developmental condition that falls under the Autism Spectrum Disorder (ASD). My mother never really discussed this with me or let me feel like I had a deficit. She supported and nurtured me. She advocated for my placement in an independent study program, where a small group of us learned differently in a class held off school grounds. Those with Asperger's may perform well in some academic subjects; however, like myself, they often struggle with social cues and nonverbal communication, such as interpreting body language, humor, or sarcasm. We also tend to fixate on specific topics or activities to an intense degree, which can interfere with daily life rather than serving as a constructive outlet. Asperger's is not a result of upbringing or parenting style, but research points to genetic factors and neurological variations in brain development (Nationwide Children's, 2021).

By high school, we had figured everything out. I had the tools needed to navigate my challenges and better understand my strengths. I began to feel more comfortable in my own skin, and slowly, things started to shift. I became more social by sophomore year, and by the time I graduated, I was even popular. My focus and determination paid off academically too—I graduated with the third-highest GPA in my class. For a while, it felt like the pieces of my life were finally coming together. But as I moved forward, I discovered that understanding neurodivergence was just one part of my journey. There were still layers to uncover.

During college, I initially resisted the idea that something else might be wrong. I was defensive, convinced that making it to college and keeping up academically meant I was fine. I didn't think I was falling apart from depression or anything like that, but as my doctor and I went through the details of my struggles, I had to face reality: there was more going on than I wanted to admit. I didn't want there to be one more thing wrong with me. But in order to get better, I had to acknowledge another diagnosis: attention deficit hyperactivity disorder (ADHD). It felt like admitting defeat, and I wasn't ready for that.

According to the Cleveland Clinic (2023), ADHD is a neurodevelopmental condition that often shows up as inattention, especially in women. These symptoms can make everyday life harder, whether it's keeping up with school, staying on track at work, or navigating social relationships. ADHD starts in childhood, but many people, like me, don't get diagnosed until much later. At its core, ADHD is about challenges with executive functioning: the mental processes that help you focus, control impulses, regulate emotions, and stay motivated. It's not about being lazy or careless; it's about your brain working differently.

After pushing past the initial dread, I tapped into the same determination my mother had shown when I was a child and began taking steps to manage my ADHD symptoms. I quickly realized that I needed guidance to organize my schedule, create study plans, and break down overwhelming assignments into smaller, manageable tasks. So I sat down with someone to map out my week, setting realistic daily goals and prioritizing tasks. Together, we tackled deadlines and broke larger projects into smaller pieces, making everything feel less daunting. Instead of letting tasks pile up until I felt paralyzed, we developed strategies to keep me ahead, like color-coded calendars, reminders, and timers to maintain focus. I also learned to balance my workload with intentional breaks to prevent burnout and found ways to stay motivated even when tasks felt tedious or frustrating. This combination of structure and accountability became the foundation that helped me not just get by but thrive during college.

I'm deeply grateful that my mother advocated for me, even if I didn't fully understand her intentions at the time. Living on campus and learning to advocate for myself, I began to see that she was trying to help me in the only way she knew how. She thought if I could just learn to blend in, I'd have a better life, an easier path. What I came to realize is that blending in doesn't work. It not only leaves you feeling like there's something inherently wrong with you but it also denies you the coping mechanisms you need to navigate life effectively.

Through it all, despite her efforts to "fix" me, my mom's strength gave me strength. She protected and fought for me, but the criticisms from family and strangers still left scars. They made me question my worth, a feeling that was exacerbated during COVID. Therapy helped me connect the dots, showing me how much those early experiences shaped the way I see myself now.

Today, because of therapy, I learned that it's okay to just be yourself—however you are, whatever you are. Life is about accepting yourself and understanding that it's okay to feel how you feel. That was my biggest takeaway: giving myself permission to be me. I also learned that I don't have to live my life trying to please everyone. So now, I don't care what anybody else thinks anymore, and that's been so freeing. And the timing was perfect. COVID had subsided, things were relatively back to normal, and I was ready to carry the strength of my mom to fight for a world where no one had to carry the weight of shame and inadequacy.

Mental Health Advocacy Post-COVID

The Center for Disease Control and Prevention (CDC, 2024) notes ADHD is one of the most common diagnoses among children in the U.S., affecting millions. They found that about 7 million kids between the ages of 3 and 17—around 11.4%—have been diagnosed with ADHD. Boys were almost twice as likely to receive a diagnosis (15%) compared to girls (8%). When you break it down by race, Black and white children had the highest rates of diagnosis (12%), while Asian children were diagnosed far less often (4%). American Indian/Alaska Native children (10%) and Native Hawaiian/Pacific Islander children (6%) were somewhere in between. Non-Hispanic children were diagnosed more often than Hispanic children, with rates of 12% and 10%, respectively. These numbers show that ADHD itself doesn't discriminate—it's everywhere. What makes the difference is access to resources and the ability to recognize the symptoms, and that gap is often shaped by race, class, and culture.

In addition to working in the rural hospital, I owned a mental health practice dispensing prescriptions. There, I saw a lot of people for ADHD medication management, and I made it a priority to advocate for the kids. One of the biggest challenges I faced, especially for Black families, was getting parents to recognize that ADHD was a legitimate issue. I'd often have parents push back, saying, "Ain't nothing wrong with my baby." And I'd get it—I lived it myself. So I'd explain, "This isn't about something being wrong with your child; this is about understanding what's happening and giving them the tools to succeed."

Then, to drive home the point, I'd break it down in a way they could relate.

"Look, you've got Jeremiah in North County, where most Black families live, and Cody in

West County, where it's more affluent and mostly white. Both kids are acting out in kindergarten, but what happens next is completely different. Jeremiah gets sent to the principal's office and written up, while Cody's teacher asks, 'What's going on at home? Are you okay'? Cody gets counseling, maybe even a diagnosis and support. Meanwhile, Jeremiah keeps acting out, and now the school's calling his mom. She's angry because she had to leave work, probably got docked pay, and Jeremiah's still being punished, maybe even suspended. It's not long before he starts hating school, and who can blame him? Cody, on the other hand, gets the help he needs. They figure out he has a learning disability, he gets medication, and starts thriving. Cody goes on to a private high school, then college, and maybe now he's a plastic surgeon. But Jeremiah? He's skipping school, getting in trouble, and maybe ends up in juvenile detention. It's not far-fetched—it's reality. The majority of people in prisons have some kind of undiagnosed mental disorder or learning disability that was never addressed."

When I explained it this way to parents, especially moms in Black communities, they'd often say, "You're right." I'd also explain that I wasn't there to push medication. I'd tell them, "Most kids with ADHD don't need meds if you clean up their diet and get them active." Natural, unprocessed whole foods and consistent physical activity go a long way. I noticed that kids who played football were fine during the season, but when it ended, their hyperactivity would spike. That showed me those kids probably needed a sport year-round because ADHD isn't about a lack of focus—it's about channeling that focus into something they care about. When they're engaged, they can thrive. It's all about giving them the right tools and opportunities. Just like my mother did for me. But no matter how far you go or how much you achieve, there will always be moments—or people—that remind you of where you started.

Chapter 6

When the 'Slow Baby' Became a Doctor

Your story is what you have, what you will always have. It is something to own.

—Michelle Obama

When my mom passed away, I was an adult with a thriving medical career and three children. The pastor of our family church, known for his humor, delivered the eulogy. He shared fond memories and lighthearted humor about my mom, even showing a picture of my parents dressed up for a night out, remarking how much they loved to have fun.

Then he began talking about how proud she was of her children. I'm the youngest of seven, with six of us still living. He listed our accomplishments: two of my brothers are engineers, another went into business, and so on. Then he said, "Even the slow baby became a doctor," and the whole church burst out laughing.

That moment caught me off guard because I thought I had done so much work to shed the label of being "slow." Not wanting to look flustered or bothered, I just stared straight ahead, refusing to meet anyone's gaze. My daughter, who was 12 at the time, leaned over and said, "Wow, you're slow?" I replied, "Apparently."

Culture

Growing up in the Black church, I often heard phrases like "too blessed to be stressed" or "we don't do therapy; that's white people shit" and saw people proudly wearing "Too Blessed to Be Stressed" on T-shirts. These weren't just sayings; they were deeply ingrained beliefs that shaped how people viewed emotional struggles and mental health. Therapy wasn't something we talked about. If you had problems, you prayed through them. Jesus was your therapist. For many, the pastor served as a counselor, even when the issues went far beyond spiritual matters.

I remember hearing women after service whisper about someone who had "gone to see a therapist." The way they said it—half pity, half judgment—made it clear that seeking professional help was seen as a failure, not strength. Even though attitudes are shifting, the stigma still lingers today.

For me, faith and therapy weren't at odds. My faith gave me strength, but therapy gave me tools. I needed both. Even still, when I started therapy after COVID, I kept it a secret, especially from people at church. I didn't want to hear, "Girl, you need to get into the upper room," or "Just pray about it." Well-meaning advice like that only reinforced the silence surrounding seeking mental health support in our community.

The church culture I grew up in didn't just overlook mental health; it sometimes worsened the shame. Depression, anxiety, and other conditions were often treated as signs of weak faith or moral failure. If someone was struggling, the answer was always to pray harder, trust God more, and rebuke the devil. Even pastors would sometimes joke about mental health, saying things like, "You just need to get right with Jesus." I never thought the comments were malicious, but the message they implied was clear: mental health issues weren't real, or if they were, they were your fault for not believing enough.

This mindset makes people feel like they have to carry their struggles alone, hiding their pain to avoid judgment. I've spoken to others who grew up in similar environments and heard their stories. Some internalized these teachings so deeply that they believed their anxiety or depression was a sin. They'd spend hours praying, reading Scripture, and trying to "fix" themselves spiritually, only to end up feeling more hopeless when nothing changed.

The stigma around mental health in the church isn't just harmful—it's dangerous. It prevents people from seeking therapy or medical treatments that could genuinely help. Faith and therapy can work together, but until we break the cycle of silence and shame, too many people will continue to suffer alone, believing their struggles are a failure of faith rather than a medical issue.

The Medical Field

The stigma around seeking mental health care isn't just present in the Black community—it's deeply rooted in the healthcare system too. In the medical field, mental health has often been treated as a weakness, something that could jeopardize your job or reputation. Doctors are expected to be healers, not patients, and the pressure to maintain that image comes at a significant cost.

The article "When Someone Great is Gone," published by Think Global Health (2023), shares the story of Dr. Lorna Breen, an ER physician who worked tirelessly in New York City during the early days of the pandemic. As the medical director of The Allen Hospital, she ended up contracting the virus herself. But, rather than taking the time to fully recover, she returned to work, still unwell, driven by her sense of duty.

The relentless pace, lack of resources, and overwhelming patient volumes took a toll on her mental health. On April 26, 2020, Lorna tragically died by suicide. She had no prior psychiatric history, but the immense pressures of her role, combined with systemic barriers to seeking help, left her struggling in silence.

Her death highlighted the urgent need to embrace the message that it's ok to not be ok and seek the help needed without fear of losing one's reputation or medical license.

Thankfully, her story led to action. The Lorna Breen Foundation, created in her honor, has championed legislation to remove invasive questions about mental health from state licensing boards and hospital credentialing processes. These reforms mark the first steps toward breaking down the culture of fear that has long prevented healthcare providers from seeking help. I am proud to be an ambassador for the foundation.

Breaking the Silence

Both the culture and the medical field taught me to stay silent, to hide my struggles, and to carry the weight of shame. But silence doesn't foster healing—it deepens the hurt. Whether it's the church telling you to pray harder or the medical field making you fear for your career, these systems perpetuate a cycle of stigma and shame.

Healing begins when we acknowledge that faith and therapy can coexist, that being a doctor doesn't mean being invincible, and that seeking help isn't weakness—it's courage. My mom gave me the tools to succeed, and I owe it to myself—and to others—to break the silence, shatter the stigma, and create space for true healing. This revelation inspired me to deliver my TEDx talk, *The Fight for Better Mental Health Care*, and to embark on a journey of advocacy.

PART 3

Realignment

Chapter 7

Breaking the Silence, Finding my Voice

There is no greater agony than bearing an untold story inside you.

—Maya Angelou

I was in my 40s when I finally became comfortable being my real, authentic self. A long-time friend even noticed how passionate I'd become about mental health—something rooted in my own journey of overcoming. I wanted others who felt what I had felt to know they could heal and live fully. She was the one who encouraged me to do a TEDx talk.

Deciding to do it wasn't easy. I carried so much shame around my past that I rarely spoke about it. I sometimes shared pieces of my story with patients struggling with mental illness, hoping it would help them feel less alone. But sharing it publicly? That felt like exposing too much. I wasn't ready to put my personal life out there for everyone to see.

Growing up, we called this "house business." And as someone on the spectrum with ADHD, being vulnerable never came naturally. In my world, vulnerability had often been met with bullying or public shame. I spent much of my life masking—presenting a version of myself that fit expectations while keeping my real emotions tightly guarded.

That's what I was taught to do. As a Black woman, I've always known I'd have to work twice as hard to get half as far. I couldn't afford to show weakness or fall short—not if I wanted to succeed. But the weight of that silence had become unbearable. I couldn't carry it anymore. Not if I wanted to heal. And certainly not if I wanted to help others.

It had become a matter of life and death. I had reached a point where I didn't want to be on this earth anymore—and I'd heard too many stories just like mine. I knew I had to share my story—especially for women and especially for Black women.

The message I shared was simple: It's okay to not be okay. It's okay to feel overwhelmed, to seek help, and to lean on others when life feels too heavy to bear alone. Yet, in crafting that message for the world, I was also speaking to myself—finally acknowledging the mental health struggles I had kept hidden for years.

When I stepped onto the red circle, I wasn't just sharing my story; it felt like using a defibrillator on my heart—shocking myself back to life after years of emotional flatline. Breaking my silence forced me to confront the wounds I had long ignored and invited others to do the same. The truth is, I hadn't shared my struggles with my family, my church, or my friends. They all learned about it alongside the rest of the world. Again, vulnerability isn't my strong suit.

But my mom had worked hard to give me the tools to navigate a world that didn't always understand me. She taught me how to read social cues, how to present myself in ways that made others comfortable, and how to adapt when I felt out of place. I used those skills to step out of my comfort zone and share my story with the world. This was the beginning of my renewed connection to medicine. I realized I did not hate being a doctor. I hated the system that was not designed for me to succeed in a healthy way. I set out to find a way to reimagine practicing medicine. I hated the culture that was being accepted as normal. I love being a doctor, and I still believe in the wonder of medicine.

Prescription: Purpose and Peace

There's a point in every healer's life when the call to care for others becomes a war against yourself. I learned that the hard way. My body kept score and nearly broke down. I was at a breaking point.

I reached that point when I stopped wanting to be here. I had given everything—my time, my energy, and my health—to medicine, and in return, I was empty. Numb. Disconnected from my kids, my purpose, and myself. I'd flatlined emotionally. And what worsened it was knowing I wasn't alone. I also had headaches and joint pain that were symptoms of an autoimmune disorder.

I'd heard too many stories just like mine. Too many Black women are cracking under the weight of invisible labor. Too many ER doctors are dying younger than they should. Too many caregivers are dying while trying to keep everyone else alive.

I had to speak up. Not just to survive, but so others could too. Because this isn't just about burnout—it's about life and death.

The Disease That Stress Creates

Stress doesn't just make you tired. It doesn't just make you irritated, foggy, or anxious. It makes you sick.

Chronic stress triggers inflammation. It dysregulates your immune system. It keeps your body stuck in fight-or-flight until it starts fighting itself. That's autoimmune disease. And who's most affected? Women. Black women.

We hold the trauma of two systems—patriarchy and racism—in our bodies. We carry the stress of caregiving, career climbing, and code-switching. We ignore symptoms until we're bedridden, then get dismissed when we seek care. And it's killing us.

Did you know that over 80% of autoimmune disease patients are women? But within that staggering statistic lies an even deeper truth: Black women are disproportionately affected, particularly by illnesses like lupus, multiple sclerosis, and scleroderma. The CDC reports that lupus is not only two to three times more common in Black women than in white women, but it is also far more deadly.

This isn't just about genetics or hormones. It's about *weathering*—a concept coined by public health researcher Dr. Arline Geronimus to describe the way chronic exposure to social, economic, and political adversity literally *wears down* the body over time (Davies, 2023). And for Black women, that weathering is relentless.

We live at the intersection of racism and sexism, carrying the weight of both. We are more likely to be primary caregivers, often single parents, tasked with holding families, workplaces, and entire communities together—all while navigating systems that were never built for us.

This isn't hypothetical for me. It's personal. I am a Black woman. A mother. A doctor. I've lived the stress, the suppression, and the constant demand to be "strong" at the expense of my own well-being. The only privilege I had was my profession. I had a medical degree, a stable income, and access to care. But even with those advantages, I *still* felt the toll of chronic stress in my body—through weight gain, fatigue, inflammation, and signs that my own system was fighting itself.

Now imagine the women who don't have the same access I had—those navigating this reality on lower incomes, without health insurance, with less societal protection.

This isn't just about individual health. It's about a systemic crisis that disguises itself as personal failure. We tell Black women to take care of themselves and then deny them the time, resources, and dignity required to do so.

The truth is, many Black women aren't getting sick because they're doing something wrong. They're getting sick because they've been doing *everything right* in a world that refuses to care for them in return.

Stress is a powerful trigger for autoimmune flares. The more stress we carry, the sicker we become. And nobody seems to talk about that part—not in medical school, not in hospitals, and definitely not at work. I remember being told, "This disease is more common in African American women." I was never told why. Was it because no one cared?

ER Medicine: The Killer Career

I used to save lives in the ER. But the truth is, the ER almost took mine. Let's look at the numbers: The average life expectancy of an ER doctor is 58.7 years. That's not a typo. That's over 15 years *less* than the general population.

And here's another one: Women live longer than men—but not if they're women in medicine. A Harvard study found that female physicians die earlier than non-physician women, primarily due to stress-related illnesses and suicide (Southwick 2025).

Let that sink in. We live less. We die younger. And we spend our lives making sure everyone else lives longer. This is why I pivoted. I'm still saving lives—just in a new way. I'm no longer putting out fires in the trauma bay. Now I prevent them from ever starting.

I Am a Stress Management Expert—Because I Had To Be

I studied stress like it was pathology. Because it is. It's behind so many of the diseases we treat every day—high blood pressure, diabetes, heart attacks, strokes, IBS, migraines, infertility, and more. Stress doesn't just hurt feelings. It breaks down your body.

I became a stress management expert the same way I became an ER doctor—because lives were on the line, including mine. Now, I teach what I had to learn the hard way:

- How to listen to your body and believe it.
- How to regulate your nervous system before it deregulates you.
- How to prioritize sleep, movement, and food as medicine.
- How to say "no" without guilt and "yes" to rest without shame.
- How to choose peace like your life depends on it—because it does.

From Burnout to Advocacy

This chapter of my life is about advocacy. Not just for physicians. Not just for Black women. But for everyone walking around silently suffering because the world told them to "push through."

I'm not pushing through anymore. I'm choosing to *live* through. And if you're reading this and it feels familiar—if your body is breaking down, your spirit is cracking, and you're afraid to say, "I'm not okay," I want you to know this:

1. You're not lazy.
2. You're not weak.
3. You're not broken.
4. You're stressed. And stress is treatable.

But only if we take it seriously. Only if we advocate like our lives depend on it, because they do.

The F.L.A.T. Framework

In my TEDx talk, I spoke about the emotional flatline, a concept I first defined in Chapter Two. This state is not about apathy or indifference; it's a defense mechanism, a survival strategy used in environments where the stakes are high. For healthcare care professionals, it begins as a protective layer, shielding us from emotional overload. But over time, that shield hardens into a barrier, numbing our ability to connect not just with patients and colleagues, but with ourselves too. The emotional flatline is one of the hidden costs of a high-stress, high-stakes profession. Burnout is a well-documented issue in health care, but the emotional flatline, the emotional toll that leads to and stems from it, remains underexplored.

Recognizing and naming this phenomenon was a pivotal step. It allowed me to boldly advocate for systemic changes to support the mental health of healthcare workers. Now, the question becomes... how do you overcome the emotional flatline?

That's where the F.L.A.T. framework comes in. Each letter in F.L.A.T. represents a critical phase in the journey back to emotional vitality and purpose. This isn't a quick fix or a one-size-fits-all solution; it's a process of unlearning survival patterns, reconnecting with your emotions, and redefining your relationship to work, rest, and self-worth. Whether you're a healthcare provider, a caregiver, or someone who has simply learned to perform through pain, this framework offers a path toward healing.

F — Feel it: Acknowledge the Numbness

You can't heal what you won't feel.

This first step is about radical honesty. Admit that something's off—even if you're still showing up to work, even if your labs are signed, your emails are answered, and your mask is on.

Recognize emotional flatlining as a survival strategy, not a personal failure. You're not broken—you're burned out.

Journaling prompt: "When did I start feeling numb?"

L — Listen Inward: Reconnect with Yourself

Flatlining disconnects us from our inner voice.

This step is about beginning the slow process of listening to your body, your emotions, and your truth. It's not about having all the answers—it's about making space to hear them.

The voice inside you didn't disappear. It just got drowned out. Your body has been whispering truths your mind learned to ignore—start listening.

Journaling prompt: "What is my body trying to tell me?"

A — Act with Intention: Reclaim Your Agency

Now we move from insight to action.

This step is about making empowered choices—on purpose, not on autopilot. You don't have to overhaul your life overnight. You just have to start.

Burnout tells you there's only one way, but coaching reminds you that you have choices.

Journaling prompt: "Where can I make one small choice for myself today?"

T — Transform: Redesign Your Life with Purpose

The final phase is about realignment.

The emotional flatline doesn't mean you've failed. It means you've felt too much, carried too much, for too long—and now, it's time to come back to yourself. Overcoming takes time and a guide such as a coach.

Purpose is the antidote to the emotional flatline. Thriving may not look like it used to—and that's not a loss, it's a sign of growth.

Journaling prompt: "What does thriving look like for me now?"

Advocacy for Physician Well-Being

Reading the YouTube comments from my TEDx reassured me that I was on the right track, so I continued my advocacy work by serving as an ambassador for the Lorna Breen Foundation and becoming a physician coach.

As an ambassador, I focus on advocating for the well-being and mental health of healthcare workers. This role involves speaking in various communities, advocating for policy changes, and promoting solutions, such as physician coaching, to tackle systemic issues such as burnout.

Burnout is a massive problem in medicine, and it doesn't happen all at once. Before full-blown burnout takes hold, there's a quieter, more insidious burnout that creeps up on us—a slow erosion of mental and emotional reserves. The problem isn't just about individuals; it's a systemic issue rooted in the very structure of how we train and treat health professionals. Residency, for example, often feels like living in an episode of *Grey's Anatomy* but without the glamour. Being on call every three days, spending 36 hours straight in the hospital, and caring for patients can be utterly exhausting. They also expect you to read journals, prepare presentations, attend morbidity and mortality conferences, and see patients in the clinic.

Then there are the 'pimp rounds,' where you're put on the spot in front of patients and colleagues. If you can't answer a question, you risk humiliation in front of an audience as well as failing your rotations. The stress of that alone is overwhelming, and nobody wants to look stupid, so the pressure never lets up. The training culture of medicine is downright toxic!

You'd think things would improve after residency, but as an attending physician, the demands don't stop. Sure, you're finally earning a substantial income, but hospitals push you to see more patients faster—an impossible task when dealing with complex cases like strokes or heart attacks. I've been told, "We need you to speed up." And I've had to respond, "I'm

sorry, but realigning a dislocated ankle joint takes time!"
As the population grows older, more obese, and sicker,
the trend worsens. It's a catch-22 because patients'
conditions are increasingly chronic and complex, but our
system is still built for quick fixes. In a society that wants
everything now, as if medicine were a Pop-Tart, the
expectations are unrealistic. We are tasked with doing
the impossible while operating at a deficit of staff and
morale.

Even when you're meeting expectations with
good patient satisfaction scores, the constant balancing
act can leave you drained. Between productivity
metrics, charting in electronic health records, and the
unrelenting demands, the pressure feels endless.

That's where physician coaching comes in, and
there's strong evidence for its effectiveness. In one
randomized clinical trial of 138 physicians, those who
received three months of coaching from professionally
trained physician peers saw a 21.6% reduction in
burnout, compared to a 2.5% increase in the control
group. Coaching also significantly reduced interpersonal
disengagement and improved professional fulfillment
and work engagement (Kiser et al., 2024).

These findings align with what I've seen firsthand: peer coaching isn't a luxury—it's a lifeline. It's an essential tool for reducing burnout and fostering well-being in high-stakes, high-stress professions like medicine. Coaching creates a safe space to call out issues, talk about them out loud, and explore solutions. I feel frustrated that I had to search for coaching on my own, but I'm grateful I eventually found it. No one ever suggested or offered it to me. I know that people in business often seek coaches. Doctors and nurses should do the same.

We can't all quit, but I understand why so many new doctors—just two or three years out of residency—want to leave the profession. I'm terrified to age in a society that devalues doctors and nurses so much. Who is going to take care of me when I am elderly? That is the very reason I fight for systemic change. Imagine dedicating four years to college, four years to medical school, three or more years to residency, and possibly additional years to a specialty, only to leave after a few years of practice. It's heartbreaking and highlights how broken the system is.

Between 2021 and 2022 alone, approximately 145,000 healthcare professionals left the workforce. Nearly half of them were physicians, with burnout being one of the leading causes (Vogel 2023). These challenges didn't start with the pandemic; it simply worsened them. Burnout among healthcare workers was already being documented. According to Moors (2023), 40% of physicians reported burnout in 2013, climbing to 51% by 2017. Even before the pandemic, studies showed that 35% to 54% of nurses and physicians were struggling with burnout. It's time we care for those who care for others. It's time to reimagine medical practice. We are in crisis mode.

Shaped by Experience

Growing up as a neurodivergent child, I often felt misunderstood. Those early experiences continue to shape how I show up today. I process the world differently than most, and that difference has made me more empathetic. I don't just focus on the problem in front of me; I think about the whole person.

When I meet with patients, I'm always asking, "What's going on in your family life?" "What's your diet like?" "Are you sleeping?" "Are you getting any exercise?" I want to understand everything that could be contributing to their health.

That's why I approach care holistically and with empathy. American medicine often fails to prioritize prevention or treat the whole person. Instead, it focuses narrowly on illness. Our system is fragmented. You go to an endocrinologist, mention a skin issue, and get referred to a dermatologist—who then tells you it's caused by diabetes. So why didn't the endocrinologist address it? Because our system treats conditions in silos instead of looking at the whole person.

It's time to move away from this reactionary model and start investing in prevention—something that's been long overlooked and underfunded. And that includes more than just physical health. Emotional and mental well-being deserve the same proactive attention.

That same mindset—seeing the whole person, not just the symptoms—is what fuels my advocacy for early diagnosis and intervention. When children who learn differently are supported early, it's not just their academic success that improves—it's their emotional resilience and self-esteem. The sooner we understand their unique needs, the sooner we can help them thrive.

Early intervention is about more than a diagnosis; it's about removing stigma. I've already seen progress in how younger generations talk about mental health, but we still need to break away from harmful labels like "slow" and build understanding from the start.

Working closely with families allows me to hear their concerns clearly. Many parents fear that a diagnosis means their child will be labeled for life or placed on medication immediately. I get it. If I were in their shoes, I'd feel the same way. That's why I take the time to explore natural, supportive approaches first. It's about making sure they feel heard and empowered every step of the way.

My experiences as a neurodivergent child have also fueled my passion for advocating for mental health in underrepresented communities. Representation matters. People of color often feel more seen and understood when their healthcare provider reflects their identity. That connection can make all the difference, especially when stigma and cultural barriers get in the way of care. I've seen firsthand how breaking down those barriers can unlock pathways to healing that might otherwise stay closed.

Advocacy for early intervention doesn't stop with children and families. It also means supporting medical students as they begin their journey. We need to have real conversations with them about boundaries, burnout, and how to structure their time in a healthy, sustainable way. No one told me during training that I could go to administration and say, "This is what I can do, and this is what I can't." But today, the culture is shifting. Administrators are more open to those conversations now, especially as nearly half of healthcare workers report plans to leave the field in the next year (Press, 2024).

By starting early, educating communities, and removing stigma, we can make mental health care more accessible and equitable for everyone. Seeking help isn't a weakness. It's strength. And it's the first step in overcoming an emotional flatline.

Chapter 8

Unwritten Prescriptions: The Silent Burden of Women in Medicine

You can't be what you can't see. We must be visible. We must be vocal. We must be vigilant in changing the face of medicine.

—Dr Joycelyn Elders

Women have always belonged in medicine. We have been healers, midwives, and caretakers for centuries—long before the title of "doctor" was bestowed upon anyone. Yet, despite making up 54.6% of students enrolled in M.D.-granting medical schools in the 2023-24 academic year (Nietzel 2024), women are leaving the profession at alarming rates. The reasons are complex, but they all point to one fundamental truth: the system wasn't built for us. We are operating in a system built by and for cisgendered white males.

The journey of women in medicine has been marked by significant milestones, pioneering individuals, and ongoing challenges. Here's an overview:

Historical Overview of Women in Medicine

Despite their longstanding contributions to health and healing, women were barred from formal medical training for much of history. It wasn't until the mid-19th century, during a wave of social reform, that they began to gain access to medical education. A pivotal moment came in 1849, when Elizabeth Blackwell graduated from Geneva Medical College, becoming the first woman in the United States to earn a medical degree. Her achievement challenged entrenched norms and opened doors for future generations of women physicians (Justin, n.d.).

In 1864, Rebecca Lee Crumpler became the first African-American woman in the United States to earn a medical degree from the New England Female Medical College. Despite the dual challenges of racial and gender discrimination, Dr. Crumpler dedicated her career to providing medical care to underserved communities (HISTORY.com Editors, 2024).

Current Challenges and Statistics on Women Leaving the Medical Profession

Despite progress, women in medicine continue to face challenges that contribute to higher attrition rates compared to their male counterparts. Research indicates that nearly 40% of women physicians either transition to part-time roles or leave the medical profession entirely within six years of completing their residencies. Factors influencing this trend include burnout, work-life balance concerns, and systemic issues within the healthcare environment. Moreover, women physicians report higher rates of burnout (54.5%) compared to men (42%) (Garvey, 2024).

While specific statistics on Black women physicians leaving the medical profession are limited, data highlights significant underrepresentation and challenges within the field. Black women comprise only

1.6% of clinical and nonclinical faculty at academic medical centers, compared to 22.9% for White women (Carr, 2020).

Additionally, Black women are often concentrated in lower-paying healthcare roles, with 92% working in positions where they are overrepresented, like licensed practical nurses, aides, and in long-term care facilities, which can impact job satisfaction and retention (Chimowitz, 2024).

Occupational Segregation of Black Women Workers in Health Care

These sources provide insights into the historical context, current challenges, and statistical data regarding women in the medical profession. While medicine prides itself on evidence-based practice, it seems to ignore the overwhelming evidence that gender disparities, systemic bias, and an outdated work culture are pushing women out. The numbers don't lie: female physicians earn less than their male counterparts, are less likely to be promoted to leadership positions, and shoulder a disproportionate share of household and caregiving responsibilities. The pressures pile up until many of us are left wondering if it's worth it. For some, the answer is no. This is a shame because medicine is better with women in it.

Numerous studies have shown that patients treated by female physicians experience better health outcomes. A 2023 Annals of Internal Medicine study found that patients under the care of female doctors had lower mortality and readmission rates compared to those treated by male physicians. Specifically, mortality was 0.47 percentage points lower—a statistically significant difference that translates to thousands of lives saved annually (UCLA Health, 2024).

Female physicians are also more likely to adhere to clinical guidelines, engage in shared decision-making, and spend more time with patients, all of which are associated with higher quality care. In fact, a study published in JAMA Internal Medicine (2017) found that elderly hospitalized patients had lower 30-day mortality and readmission rates when treated by female internists.

Medicine is not only more compassionate with women—it's more effective, more equitable, and more patient-centered.

The Gender Pay Gap in Medicine

Medicine may wear the mask of meritocracy, but behind the scenes, gender pay disparities reveal a different story. Year after year, studies show that women doctors earn significantly less than men—even when controlling for specialty, work hours, and experience (Whaley et al., 2021). A 2022 JAMA study found that over a 40-year career, women physicians make an average of $2 million less than their male counterparts. In some specialties, that gap grows even wider.

In my own career, I've seen these inequities play out firsthand. Early on, I never thought to question my salary or negotiate for better pay. Like many women physicians, I assumed the system was fair—that if I worked hard and proved myself, my compensation would reflect my value. It wasn't until I started having candid conversations with colleagues that I realized just how much I was leaving on the table. Two experiences stand out vividly.

First, a white female colleague, someone who had been in the field longer than I had, advised me to demand loan repayment and ask for higher pay. Initially,

I hesitated, plagued by imposter syndrome and the fear of being seen as "difficult." Negotiating felt foreign, almost taboo. But with her encouragement, I pushed past that discomfort, and to my surprise, I successfully secured both loan repayment and a significant salary increase.

Then, when I was considering a new position, my ER doctor friend Randi urged me to ask for a $75,000 sign-on bonus. The very idea terrified me. The voice in my head whispered, You should just be grateful for the offer. What if they think you're greedy? What if they rescind the offer altogether? But Randi believed in my worth, even when I doubted it myself. With her encouragement, I asked, and to my amazement, they agreed.

These moments were transformative. Not only did they have immediate financial benefits, but they also reshaped how I saw myself in the medical field. I learned that negotiation wasn't about being pushy or ungrateful. It was about knowing my worth and advocating for it. That realization changed the way I approached my career, and it's one of the key lessons I now share with women in high-achieving roles.

But the fact that I needed mentorship to learn these things speaks to a larger issue. Women aren't taught to negotiate. We aren't told, "You should ask for more. You deserve better." Instead, we are conditioned to accept what we're given and be grateful for the opportunity. Meanwhile, our male counterparts negotiate aggressively from the start, setting themselves up for better pay, better contracts, and better benefits.

This isn't an issue of individual failure—it's a systemic problem. Studies show that even when women do negotiate, we are penalized for it. We're seen as "aggressive" or "demanding," while men who ask for the same things are viewed as confident and competent.

With the mentorship and encouragement of my colleagues, I didn't just navigate the system to negotiate for a higher salary; I stepped into leadership. That willingness to advocate for myself led to me becoming a medical director, a role I once thought was out of reach. Now, I use my experience to help other women break through the barriers that hold them back.

The Invisible Labor of Women Physicians

Women take on an enormous amount of invisible labor, both in and outside of the hospital. Yet, despite these benefits to patients, the additional labor that we perform is rarely acknowledged or rewarded. We are disproportionately expected to take on extra tasks that do not lead to promotions, such as serving on committees, mentoring younger colleagues, or being the "go-to" person for emotional support among staff. While male doctors are more likely to receive high-profile leadership opportunities, the tasks that female physicians are saddled with rarely advance their careers. This contributes to gender disparities in leadership, as women are kept from the networking and research opportunities that pave the way for promotions.

Then there's the burden outside the hospital. We're also mothers, daughters, and caregivers. Even in households where both parents work full-time, we are often expected to be the primary caretakers, bearing the mental load of managing childcare, scheduling doctor's appointments, helping with homework, and keeping the household running. What's more troubling is that this imbalance persists even when women are the primary or sole breadwinners. For some, this expectation becomes overwhelming, forcing many to opt for part-time positions, transition into lower-paying specialties, or leave medicine altogether.

Invisible labor and unequal duties stem from outdated societal norms, but they also offer an opportunity to undo the conditioning many of us have internalized. The first step lies in asserting our needs and setting boundaries, but the rest involves retraining our families, our partners, and society at large. Also, we must teach our children that domestic labor isn't gendered and model equitable partnerships at home if we want to see sustainable change.

The cumulative effect of these labor disparities leads to higher burnout rates among women physicians. A 2022 American Medical Association survey found that 57% of female doctors reported experiencing at least one symptom of burnout, compared to 47% of male doctors. The reasons are clear: women physicians are paid less, work harder, have fewer resources, and are less likely to be promoted. They also face constant scrutiny and higher expectations while receiving less respect in the workplace.

If you're a doctor, nurse, anesthesiologist, etc., you deserve fair pay, leadership opportunities, and a workplace that respects your contributions. It's time to advocate for yourself, set boundaries, and take control of your career. The system may not have been built for us, but that doesn't mean we can't reshape it, one career at a time.

Why Women Are Leaving Medicine

For many of us, it's not a question of whether we love medicine. It's a question of whether medicine loves us back. We are underpaid, overworked, and forced to choose between career advancement and personal well-being. We are told that working harder will eventually pay off, but the truth is, the system was never designed to reward us equally.

Women in medicine aren't leaving because we can't handle it. We're leaving because the system refuses to change for us.

Chapter 9

Reclaiming the White Coat

I am no longer accepting the things I cannot change. I am changing the things I cannot accept.

—Angela Davis

Being a female doctor is stressful. I sometimes wonder which is harder: being a female in medicine or being Black. The truth is, both come with layers of bias and disrespect. Sometimes it's subtle, sometimes it's blatant, but it's always exhausting. And we're expected to just take it.

I cannot tell you how many times I've been called "hon" or "sweetheart." I nod and say, "It's Dr. Buchanan." I get asked if my husband is ok sharing me with the hospital. I get asked if my kids are ok. They are exceptional, by the way. They're well-adjusted honor students who think their mother is a badass and boss bitch (their words). After the divorce, one doctor asked how I could afford to take care of the kids. I'm doing fine on the six-figure salary, thank you for asking. Then there are the moments that are so absurd, they'd be funny if they weren't so insulting.

I recall going into the patient room of a middle-aged white male in my white coat and saying, "I am Dr. Buchanan." I examined him and gave orders to the nurse; I even did a rectal exam. As I was leaving the room, the patient asked when the doctor was coming in. I do not know about you, but if someone comes into my ER room and puts a finger in any hole in my body, they had better be a doctor! The fact that he could not conceive that I was a doctor *after* I introduced myself as Dr. Buchanan and did all the things doctors do blows my mind. This happened just last year.

Too many of us are taught to be grateful for what we're given. We're told to grin and bear the disrespect of patients, the bias of colleagues, and the unfair treatment baked into the system. We're told to work harder, be patient, and trust that we'll be rewarded. But that's not how change happens. Change happens when we make it happen.

We know what needs to be done: (1) pay transparency and equity; (2) parental leave and work-life balance; (3) diversity in leadership; and (4) mentorship and sponsorship.

Pay transparency and equity. Salary secrecy benefits institutions, not physicians. Women deserve to know where they stand and to be compensated fairly for their work.

Parental leave and work-life balance. The culture of overwork in medicine is not sustainable. Some real solutions include paid parental leave, flexible scheduling, and reasonable workloads.

Diversity in leadership. More women in leadership means enacting policies that reflect the realities of our lives. It means a culture shift, not just inclusion in name only.

Mentorship and sponsorship. Women physicians need more than advice—we need advocates who will open doors, recommend us for promotions, and ensure that our voices are heard.

Even when we understand what needs to be done, taking action isn't always easy. Many of us were never taught to negotiate or advocate for ourselves. The idea of stepping into leadership or asking for better pay can feel uncomfortable when we've been conditioned to accept what we're given.

Case Studies: Women Physicians Taking Charge of Their Careers

Despite the challenges, many women in medicine are not walking away; they are reclaiming their power, redefining success, and building careers on their own terms. By negotiating for what they deserve, stepping into leadership, and creating opportunities beyond traditional hospital settings, these women are proving that they don't have to accept the status quo.

I've witnessed the OB-GYN who restructured her schedule to finally breathe, choosing leadership and policy over burnout so she could be present for her kids *and* her calling.

I've seen the ER doc who spent years being overlooked, underpaid, and underestimated finally stand up, negotiate her worth, and rise into a leadership role where she now protects the well-being of others.

I've walked beside the surgeon who left a prestigious institution that refused to see her value and watched her build a private practice rooted in purpose, mentorship, and equity.

These aren't hypotheticals. These are real physicians. Real women who refused to settle for less. Women who bet on themselves and won. These women turned stress into strategy, burnout into boundaries, and purpose into profit.

You can, too. Your career, your boundaries, and your dreams are worth protecting. With clarity, intention, and support, anything is possible. The path forward may not be easy, but it is within reach for anyone who dares to pursue it.

Redefining Success in Medicine

Women in medicine are at a crossroads. The profession is losing talented physicians, not because we lack the skills or resilience to thrive, but because the system refuses to adapt. We are overworked, underpaid, and often forced to choose between career advancement and personal well-being. Many of us reach a breaking point, wondering if staying in medicine is even sustainable.

That's where physician coaching makes a difference. Coaching isn't about motivation or vague encouragement; it's about strategy. It creates a space to set goals, establish boundaries, and make career decisions with clarity and confidence. Coaching provides the structure and support that many of us never received in our medical training, such as negotiating for better pay, stepping into leadership roles, and creating balance in a profession that always demands more than we can safely give.

I didn't always understand the value of coaching. I believed that if I worked hard, everything would fall into place. But over time, I realized that hard work alone wasn't enough. I needed to learn how to advocate for myself, how to negotiate, and how to structure my career in a way that worked for me, not just for the hospital system. Coaching provided me with those tools.

How Coaching Changed My Career

At my lowest point, I turned to therapy; I had never considered coaching. Therapy helped some. I was no longer suicidal, but I still felt stuck and disconnected from any real sense of hope. My therapist was kind and well-intentioned, but she had never been a physician. She couldn't fully grasp the weight I was carrying. I'm reminded of the old saying, "It takes one to know one." While that saying is usually referencing an asshole, in this instance, I am referencing being a doctor.

There's a special kind of crazy required to be a doctor. Only another physician could truly understand what I was going through. Therapy was the beginning of my healing; it helped me name what I was feeling and reminded me that I wasn't alone. But it was working with a physician coach that shifted everything. She helped me see that my depression was a predictable outcome of a system that doesn't support us. And that I had options. I didn't have to keep practicing medicine the way I had been. I could choose a path that felt healthier, more joyful, and more aligned with who I was becoming. I was all in. Now, all I want to do is help other women, especially other women doctors, understand that sometimes, stress is optional. You can choose better. You can choose purpose. You can choose joy.

The Coach Who Helped Me Breathe Again

I didn't realize how deep I was in it until I couldn't feel anything anymore. I was showing up for shifts. Smiling on Zoom calls. Writing notes. Giving advice. Signing off on labs. From the outside, I looked fine. But inside, I was running on fumes—no, less than fumes. I was empty. Numb. Like I was watching my own life from the outside, unable to reach myself.

I had become that doctor, the one everyone relied on, but no one really checked on. And to be honest, I didn't know how to ask for help. I thought I was just "tired." That maybe a weekend off or a new planner would fix it. It didn't.

What saved me wasn't a vacation or a new job. It was a coach. Not just any coach—a physician coach. Someone who knew what it was like to be me. Someone who had worn the white coat, who had charted at 2 a.m., who had cried in the supply closet and smiled for a patient five minutes later. She didn't just understand medicine. She understood me.

I remember our first session. She asked me, "What do you want?," and I didn't know how to answer. Not what my patients wanted. Not what my hospital wanted. Not what my kids or my husband or my colleagues wanted. What did *I* want?

It took me weeks to even hear my own voice again. She helped me find it. Session by session, she peeled back the layers of guilt, of fear, of obligation. She held space for my anger. My sadness. My exhaustion. And she didn't try to "fix" me. She reminded me I wasn't broken; I was burnt out. There's a difference.

With her help, I learned how to set boundaries without guilt. How to say no with love. How to put myself first. She helped me believe that staying in medicine didn't have to mean sacrificing my sanity.

- That I could serve and still have a life.
- That I could lead and still rest.
- That I could heal others without destroying myself.

That coach didn't just help me get through burnout. She helped me rise from it. And then I realized I wasn't alone. In fact, I was one of many.

Conclusion
A New Definition of Healing

As a Black physician, I am not just treating patients—I am dismantling structures. Racism is a system, and we must be courageous enough to name it, challenge it, and work to dismantle it in every exam room and boardroom.

—Dr. Camara Phyllis Jones

As physicians, we're taught to recognize the signs of cardiac arrest. We know how to respond when a heart stops. But what we're rarely taught is how to respond when the spark that once fueled our purpose begins to dim and the emotional toll of this work catches up to us.

That's what this book has been about: learning how to recognize, name, and recover from the emotional flatline. I wrote this not as a theoretical guide, but from lived experience. I've sat in the silence of a call room after watching a patient die. I've driven home through empty streets wondering if I'd ever feel normal again. I've been praised for my strength in one moment and called a racial slur in the next. And for too long, I thought that was just part of the job.

But what I've come to understand—and what I hope this book has shown you—is that surviving is not the same as living. We cannot continue to pour from an empty cup, to heal others while neglecting ourselves, or to carry the unspoken belief that sacrifice is a requirement for legitimacy in medicine.

The white coat is not supposed to cost us our peace. It is meant to represent healing—and that includes healing for ourselves. What I found through coaching, and what ultimately helped me reconnect with my purpose, was the realization that we get to define what success in medicine looks like. We don't have to do it the way it's always been done. We can build something different.

Living with purpose is not about quitting medicine. It's about practicing it in a way that honors your humanity, your health, and your unique gifts. For some, that might mean stepping into leadership. For others, it means restructuring your practice or reclaiming time for family. For me, it meant creating a space for other women to heal, connect, and rebuild on their terms.

If you've seen yourself in these pages—if you've felt the weight, the weariness, the quiet numbness—I want you to know there's more beyond this moment. There is a way forward. And you don't have to find it alone.

The Path Forward

The healthcare system is at a critical juncture. We cannot afford to lose one more nurse, one more physician, one more healer. If we want a sustainable future in medicine, we must change the culture, starting with helping the helpers. That's why I'm not just a believer in coaching. I'm a testament to what's possible when we give our healers the help they give to others.

Change is happening. More women are speaking up. More of us are refusing to settle. I see it in my own journey, in my colleagues, and in the physicians who are stepping into leadership and redefining what success in medicine looks like.

If you've ever felt stuck, undervalued, overwhelmed, or unsure about your next steps, coaching can help. It helped me. But even more powerful than coaching—what I now live and breathe—is purpose.

Purpose: The Prescription That Saved My Life

For years, I gave everything I had to medicine. To my patients. To the hospital. To a system that took and took but rarely gave back. On paper, I was successful. But inside? I was exhausted, burnt out, and emotionally flatlined. Coaching helped me name what I was feeling. But it was purpose that brought me back to life.

Purpose gave me clarity when everything felt blurry. It reminded me of who I was and why I started this journey in the first place. With that clarity came conviction. And with conviction came confidence.

When you know who you are and why you do what you do, you stop looking for external validation.

You stop shrinking. You stop waiting for someone to give you permission. You show up fully as yourself.

Purpose isn't about titles or degrees. It's about impact. And once you align your life and work with that impact in mind, burnout doesn't stand a chance.

I'm not surviving anymore. I'm living in purpose. On purpose. And I want that for you, too.

Let's Do This Together

If you're ready to reclaim your joy, rediscover your power, and start living in alignment with your purpose, I'd love to support you. Whether you're a doctor, nurse, executive, entrepreneur—or someone who's just tired of living in survival mode—there's a space here for you.

The StrongHer Purpose Circle is more than a membership. It's a movement. It's a space for women who are done shrinking themselves to fit into systems that were never built for them. In this community, we live boldly, we heal together, and we support each other with intention. Members receive monthly coaching, access to expert guest speakers, practical resources, and, most importantly, a sisterhood that holds space for who you are and who you're becoming. To be added to the Circle, visit bit.ly/4cRQRn3; you'll also get the free guide, The StrongHER Method™: 10 Ways to Banish Stress for Good.

This group isn't about simply surviving the demands of life and medicine; it's about reclaiming your time, your voice, and your purpose. Burnout is not your destiny. You can recover from an emotional flatline. Purpose is your power. And you don't have to walk this path alone. You deserve more than just getting by; you deserve to live in purpose, on purpose. And I'm here to support you every step of the way.

Bibliography

Agency for Healthcare Research and Quality. 2017. "Physician Burnout." Ahrq.gov. July 2017. https://www.ahrq.gov/prevention/clinician/ahrq-works/burnout/index.html.

American Medical Association and American Medical Association. "New Data Sheds Light on the Gender Gap in Physician Burnout." American Medical Association, September 12, 2023. https://www.ama-assn.org/practice-management/physician-health/new-data-sheds-light-gender-gap-physician-burnout.

Carr, Rotonya M. 2020. "Reflections of a Black Woman Physician-Scientist." Journal of Clinical Investigation 130 (11): 5624–25. https://doi.org/10.1172/JCI144525.

CBC. 2022. "Are We Mislabeling Our Trauma? Why Dr. Gabor Maté Believes We Need to Change the Way We Think about Pain," November 25. https://www.cbc.ca/radio/thenextchapter/are-

we-mislabeling-our-trauma-why-dr-gabor-mat
%C3%A9-believes-we-need-to-change-the-way-
we-think-about-pain-1.6661540.

CDC. 2024. "Data and Statistics on ADHD."
    Attention-Deficit / Hyperactivity Disorder
    (ADHD). CDC. November 19, 2024.
    https://www.cdc.gov/adhd/data/index.html.

Chimowitz, Hannah. 2024. "Occupational Segregation
    of Black Women Workers in Health Care -
    National Employment Law Project." National
    Employment Law Project. December 23, 2024.
    https://www.nelp.org/insights-research/occup
    ational-segregation-of-black-women-workers-i
    n-health-care/.

Cleveland Clinic. 2023. "ADHD in Women:
    Symptoms, Diagnosis & Treatment."
    Cleveland Clinic. February 15, 2023.
    https://my.clevelandclinic.org/health/diseases/
    24741-adhd-in-women.

Cordova, Pamela B., Mary L. Johansen, Irina B.
    Grafova, Suzanne Crincoli, Joseph Prado, and
    Monika Pogorzelska-Maziarz. 2022. "Burnout
    and Intent to Leave during COVID-19: A

Cross-Sectional Study of New Jersey Hospital Nurses." Journal of Nursing Management 30 (6). https://doi.org/10.1111/jonm.13647.

Davies, Dave. 2023. "How Poverty and Racism 'Weather' the Body, Accelerating Aging and Disease." NPR. March 28, 2023. https://www.npr.org/sections/health-shots/2023/03/28/1166404485/weathering-arline-geronimus-poverty-racism-stress-health.

Garvey, Georgia. "Despite Drop in Burnout, Women Physicians Still Feeling Burden." American Medical Association. August 6, 2024. https://www.ama-assn.org/practice-management/physician-health/despite-drop-burnout-women-physicians-still-feeling-burden?utm_source=chatgpt.com.

HISTORY.com Editors. 2024. "Rebecca Lee Crumpler Becomes First Black Woman to Earn a Medical Degree | March 1, 1864 | HISTORY." HISTORY. February 26, 2024. https://www.history.com/this-day-in-history/march-1/rebecca-lee-crumpler-first-black-woman-to-earn-a-medical-degree.

Justin, Meryl S. n.d. "'The Entry of Women into
        Medicine in America' | Elizabeth Blackwell |
        HWS." Www.hws.edu.
        https://www.hws.edu/about/history/elizabeth-
        blackwell/entry-of-women-into-medicine.aspx.

Kiser, Stephanie B., J. David Sterns, Po Ying Lai, Nora
        K. Horick, and Kerri Palamara. 2024.
        "Physician Coaching by Professionally Trained
        Peers for Burnout and Well-Being." JAMA
        Network Open 7 (4): e245645.
        doi:10.1001/jamanetworkopen.2024.5645.

Martin, Brendan, Nicole Kaminski-Ozturk, Charlie
        O'Hara, and Richard Smiley. 2023.
        "Examining the Impact of the COVID-19
        Pandemic on Burnout and Stress among U.S.
        Nurses." Journal of Nursing Regulation 14
        (1): 4–12.
        https://doi.org/10.1016/s2155-8256(23)00063
        -7.

Mensik, Hailey. 2022. "Over 200,000 Healthcare
        Workers Quit Jobs Last Year." Healthcare Dive.
        October 26, 2022.

https://www.healthcaredive.com/news/covid-p
andemic-healthcare-burnout-providers-quit-jo
bs/634946/.

Moors, Sarah. 2023. "Beyond Burnout: Why
Physicians Are Leaving Their Jobs in Droves."
Digital Health Insights, October 23.
https://www.dhinsights.org/news/beyond-bur
nout.

Nationwide Children's. 2021. "Asperger's Syndrome."
Www.nationwidechildrens.org. 2021.
https://www.nationwidechildrens.org/conditio
ns/aspergers-syndrome.

NCSBN. 2023. "NCSBN Research Projects
Significant Nursing Workforce Shortages and
Crisis." National Council of State Boards of
Nursing. April 13, 2023.
https://www.ncsbn.org/news/ncsbn-research-
projects-significant-nursing-workforce-shortag
es-and-crisis.

"New Data Sheds Light on the Gender Gap in
Physician Burnout." 2023. American Medical
Association. September 12, 2023.

https://www.ama-assn.org/practice-manageme
nt/physician-health/new-data-sheds-light-gend
er-gap-physician-burnout.

Nietzel, Michael T. 2024. "Women Dominating
Enrollments in Health Care Professional
Programs." Forbes. December 27, 2024.
https://www.forbes.com/sites/michaeltnietzel/
2024/12/27/women-dominating-enrollments-i
n-health-care-professional-programs/.

"Occupational Segregation of Black Women Workers
in Health Care - National Employment Law
Project." 2025. National Employment Law
Project. April 2, 2025.
https://www.nelp.org/insights-research/occup
ational-segregation-of-black-women-workers-i
n-health-care/?utm_source=chatgpt.com.

Press. 2024. "Invenias Product Roadmap Session."
Staffing Industry News, Events, Blog,
Resources, Marketing | Staffing Hub. January
23, 2024.
https://staffinghub.com/press-releases/nearly-h
alf-of-healthcare-workers-considering-leaving-t
heir-jobs-this-year-eyeing-temporary-workc/.

Southwick, Ron. 2025. "Women Have Longer
Lifespans than Men, but Women Doctors
Don't Have That Edge." OncLive. March 8,
2025.
https://www.chiefhealthcareexecutive.com/vie
w/women-have-longer-lifespans-than-men-but-
women-doctors-don-t-have-that-edge.

Tsugawa, Yusuke, Anupam B. Jena, Jose F. Figueroa, E.
John Orav, Daniel M. Blumenthal, and Ashish
K. Jha. 2017. "Comparison of Hospital
Mortality and Readmission Rates for Medicare
Patients Treated by Male vs Female Physicians."
JAMA Internal Medicine 177 (2): 206.
https://doi.org/10.1001/jamainternmed.2016.
7875.

UCLA Health. "Treatment From Female Doctors
Leads to Lower Mortality and Hospital
Readmission Rates," April 22, 2024.
https://www.uclahealth.org/news/release/treat
ment-female-doctors-leads-lower-mortality-and
-hospital.

Vogel, Susanna. 2023. "Healthcare Worker Exodus Continued through 2022, New Data Shows." Healthcare Dive. October 17, 2023. https://www.healthcaredive.com/news/healthcare-worker-exodus-physician-burnout-definitive/696769/.

Weill, David. 2024. "Women Doctors Are More Effective. We Need More of Them." Los Angeles Times. October 4, 2024. https://www.latimes.com/opinion/story/2024-10-04/women-doctor-medicine-healthcare-sexism-equality.

Whaley, Christopher M., Tina Koo, Vineet M. Arora, Ishani Ganguli, Nate Gross, and Anupam B. Jena. 2021. "Female Physicians Earn an Estimated $2 Million Less than Male Physicians over a Simulated 40-Year Career." Health Affairs 40 (12): 1856–64. https://doi.org/10.1377/hlthaff.2021.00461.

"When Someone Great Is Gone | Think Global Health." 2023. Think Global Health. April 26, 2023.

https://www.thinkglobalhealth.org/article/when-someone-great-gone.